FELT DOGS

Mitsuki ☆ Hoshi

Laurence King Publishing

D1445218

Materials supplied by:

 Hamanaka
  Kyoto Head Office, 2-3 Hanazonoyabunoshita-cho, Ukyo-ku, Kyoto-shi
  ☎ 075-463-5151
  Tokyo Branch, 1-11-10 Nihonbashi Hama-cho, Chuo-ku, Tokyo
  ☎ 03-3864-5151
  http://www.hamanaka.co.jp

Original Japanese edition:

Publisher ························· Sunao Onuma
Book design ······················ Gen Watanabe
Photography ······················ Yasuo Nagumo
Styling ·························· Kumiko Nagumo
Tracing ·························· Kumiko Kurokawa
Proofreading ····················· Emiko Horiguchi
Planning support ·················· Shingo Taneda (Livretech)
Editing ·························· Tomoe Horie
                            Norie Hirai (Bunka Publishing Bureau)

English edition:

Translated from the Japanese by ··· Andy Walker
Technical consultant ··············· Chika Ito
Design and typesetting ············ Mark Holt
Commissioning editor ············ Sarah Batten
Project editor····················· Gaynor Sermon

Mitsuki ☆ Hoshi

Arts & crafts writer:

Mitsuki Hoshi has published on a wide range of arts and crafts in books and magazines, and her distinctive adorable-looking soft toys enjoy great popularity.

Her trademark is the ability to make anything at all from a piece of wool, from animals to food, as epitomized by the crocheted stuffed animals in *Ami Ami Dogs*.

Now, in this book, she turns her hand to producing her trademark crocheted dogs in wool felt.

Her major publications include *Ami Ami Dogs: Seriously Cute Crochet, Ami Ami Dogs 2: More Seriously Cute Crochet, The Night Before Christmas in Crochet,* and *Dog Sweaters and Accessories.*

http://hoshi-mitsuki.com/

LAURENCE KING

Published in 2014 by Laurence King Publishing Ltd
361-373 City Road
London EC1V 1LR
United Kingdom
Tel: +44 20 7841 6900
Fax: +44 20 7841 6910
email: enquiries@laurenceking.com
www.laurenceking.com

Copyright © Mitsuki Hoshi 2010
All rights reserved.
Original Japanese edition published by EDUCATIONAL FOUNDATION BUNKA GAKUEN BUNKA PUBLISHING BUREAU.

This English edition is published by arrangement with EDUCATIONAL FOUNDATION BUNKA GAKUEN BUNKA PUBLISHING BUREAU, Tokyo in care of Tuttle-Mori Agency Inc., Tokyo

All rights reserved. No part of this publication may be reproduced or transmitted in any form or by any means, electronic or mechanical, including photocopy, recording or any information storage and retrieval system, without prior permission in writing from the publisher.

A catalogue record for this book is available from the British Library.

ISBN: 978-1-78067-339-4

Printed in China

FELT DOGS

Create your own felt dogs
by working wool felt with
a needle.

Make your favorite dogs
and set them in the pose
of your choice.

Contents

HOW TO MAKE THE DOGS

LET'S GET STARTED!

MINIATURE DACHSHUND

...... → page 48

WELSH CORGI

• • • • • • → page 50

MINIATURE SCHNAUZER

• • • • • • → page 52

PUG

• • • • • • → page 54

CHIHUAHUA

LABRADOR RETRIEVER

• • • • • → page 58

SHIBA

• • • • • → page 60

MALTESE

• • • • • • → page 62

BEAGLE

• • • • • • → page 64

TOY POODLE

• • • • • • → page 66

BOSTON TERRIER

• • • • • •⟶ page 68

MINIATURE PINSCHER

●●●●●● ➞ page 70

HOW TO MAKE THE DOGS

 FELT DOGS

General instructions

Here we demonstrate the basic method for creating the dogs by making a Welsh Corgi in a standing pose.

These general instructions apply to any of the breeds, so please refer to them for whichever dog you are making.

Actual-size photographs are included on the instruction page for each dog so that you can take exact measurements.

The felt wool weights provided on the instruction pages are intended as a rough guide.

When felt wool is worked by jabbing with a specially designed needle, the fine fibers in the wool become entwined to create felt.

More jabs produce firmer felt, and fewer jabs leave it softer, so sculpt the wool with the needle until it reaches the desired firmness.

Always use a felting mat on which to jab the wool, and bring the needle out in the same orientation as you jabbed it in.

* Be careful not to prick yourself with the needle.

Wool felt

These are the wool felts that are used in this book. The materials are 100% merino wool.

Wadding

These are the felts that we use for the filling. The wool is already shaped in wads, so it will mat together nicely with just a little needling, and you can then lay the wool felt on top.

Felting needles

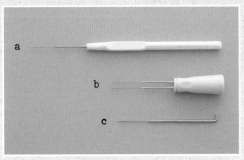

Felting needles are specially constructed so that you need only jab the needle into the fabric for the fibers to interlock and create felt.

a With a handle for ease of holding and to prevent hand fatigue.
b With two barbs, for nimble movement and a speedy finish.
c Standard felting needle.

Other supplies

Tools

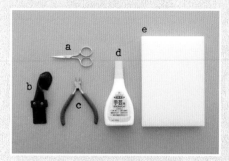

a   Thread-cutting scissors: You will need sharp scissors with pointed ends for cutting wool felt and embroidery thread and for trimming to a finish.

b   A finger cot designed for felting: To protect your fingers when you are using a felting needle.

c   Nippers: To cut the shaft off the nose piece.

d   Craft glue: Choose a quick-drying glue that is clear when dry.

e   Felting mat: A mat to use for felting the wool with a needle.

How to use a finger cot

Wear the finger cot on the hand in which you are holding the wool (whether left or right) to protect a wide area of your finger, from base to tip.

Embroidery thread and needles

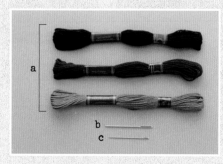

a   No. 25 embroidery thread: To embroider the mouth.

b   Wool needle: To make the holes for inserting the eyes.

c   Embroidery needle: Thread with embroidery thread to embroider the mouth.

Eyes and mouth

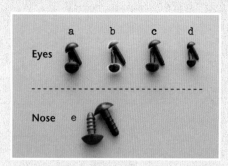

a   Solid eyes (black) ¼ in (6 mm)
b   Flat eyes (clear) ¼ in (6 mm)
c   Flat eyes (light brown) ¼ in (6 mm)
d   Solid eyes (black) ⅛ in (4 mm)
e   Nose (black, brown) ⅜ in (9 mm)

Preparing flat eyes (clear)

Use a correction pen to paint the reverse white and outline the blacks of the eyes.

Names of the parts

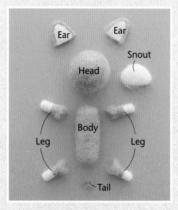

Ear Ear Snout Head Body Leg Leg Tail

 ## Make the head

1 Place a square of wadding of around 2¾ in (7 cm) on the felting mat.

2 Fold one third of the length underneath.

3 Fold again.

4 Mat firmly by jabbing with a (two-barb) needle.

5 Fold about one third from the left and jab with the needle.

6 Fold from the right and jab with the needle.

Continued overleaf →

Instructions

7 Roll into a ball with your hands.

8 Jab with the needle to make the shape even rounder.

9 The filling for the head will look like this when finished, with a diameter of 1 in (2.5 cm).

10 Tear the beige wool felt into thin strips.

11 Place the filling for the head on the wool felt.

12 Wrap the wool felt around the head filling, jabbing with the needle.

13 Jab evenly, wrapping in such a way that the head filling is hidden from view.

14 The finished head will look like this, with a diameter of 1⅛ in (3 cm).

15 Add the stripe to the head. Place some white wool felt in the center of the head end and jab with the needle.

16 The stripe will look like this when finished, with a width of ¼ in (6 mm) x length of ¾ in (2 cm).

Make the body

1 Make the body filling with wadding and wrap in beige wool felt (see p. 35 to 36) The body is ⅜ in (1.5 cm) in diameter x 1⅝ in (4.2 cm) in length.

2 Jab evenly, wrapping in such a way that the body filling is hidden from view (see p. 35 to 36).

3 Make into a rounded shape so the filling can't be seen at the tail end (it's OK if it is visible at the head end). The body is ¾ in (2 cm) in diameter x 1 ¾ in (4.5 cm) length.

4 Make the neck area. Add some white wool felt at the head end and jab with the needle.

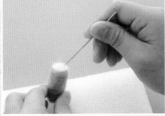

5 Arrange into a neatly rounded shape, in the same way as the tail end.

6 Twist some white wool felt into a long, thin strand with your fingers and position it around the edge of the neck.

7 Jab all the way round to make the edge stand out.

8 The body will look like this when finished.

Instructions

 Make the legs

1 Make the filling for the legs. Tear the white wool into thin tufts. The legs are only small, so you do not have to use wadding.

2 Fold in two lengthways, and then fold again.

3 Jab with the needle to form into a cylinder shape, ¼ in (6 mm) in diameter x 2 in (5 cm) in length.

4 Holding lengthways, jab the end of the leg.

5 It does not matter if the end that you attach to the body is wispy.

6 Place the leg filling on some beige wool felt, leaving around ¼ in (6 mm) showing at the foot of the leg.

7 Jab evenly, wrapping in such a way that the leg filling is hidden from view (see p. 36).

8 The leg will look like this when it has been wrapped in wool felt.

9 Make the foot. Tear some white wool into a thin tuft and wrap it around the foot.

10 Wrapping the leg in the white wool felt, jab evenly to shape.

11 The leg with the finished foot will look like this.

12 Cut the leg ¾ in (2 cm) from the end.

13 The leg will look like this when it's finished, ⅜ in (9 mm) in diameter x ¾ in (2 cm) in length.

4 Attach the legs

1 Place the leg against the body and jab the join with the needle.

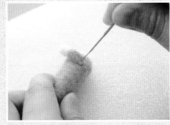

2 Jab thoroughly enough to flatten out the join.

3 Add some beige wool felt to the join.

Continued overleaf ⇒

Instructions

 Jab thoroughly to blend into the body.

5 Jab the other three legs in the same way.

6 The body will look like this when the legs are attached.

5 Make and attach the tail

1 Jab a piece of beige wool felt thoroughly, shaping it into a ball.

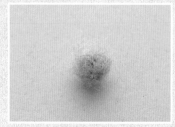

2 The tail will look like this when finished, with a diameter of ¼ in (6 mm).

3 Attach the tail to the rear. Jab around the tail area, being careful not to squash the roundness at the center of the tail.

 The body will look like this when the tail has been attached.

6 Make the snout

 Jab a piece of white wool felt into shape, folding it on the felting mat as you work.

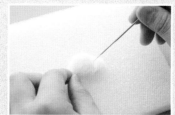

 Jab thoroughly to shape the snout.

 Hold the wool felt in your hand and jab to sculpt the edges.

 The snout will look like this when finished, with a thickness of ⅜ in (9 mm).

7 Attach the nose

 Cut the shaft of the nose piece with the nippers.

 The nose piece with the shaft cut off. You will use the flat part, as shown here.

 Take a small amount of glue on a wool needle (or toothpick), and apply it to the back of the nose.

 Stick the nose onto the snout.

. Instructions

8 Embroider the mouth

1 Embroider with dark brown embroidery thread (2-ply). Thread through the back and out under the nose.

2 Insert the needle diagonally under the nose.

3 Push the needle out around ⅛ in (4 mm) diagonally above the nose.

4 Insert the needle at the position shown in **2**.

5 Embroider the other side in the same way.

9 Attach the snout

1 Attach the snout to the head, jabbing so that the bottom ¼ in (6 mm) of the stripe is hidden.

2 Jab around the edge of snout to secure it in place.

3 Jab the center of the snout lightly so that it does not get squashed.

4

The head will look like this when the snout has been attached.

10 Attach the eyes

1 Use a wool needle to jab sockets at the positions where the eyes will go.

2 Dab a small amount of glue onto the tip of the eye pieces and push them into the sockets.

3 The head will look like this when the eyes are attached.

11 Make and attach the ears

1 Shape a piece of beige wool felt to the actual-size pattern for the ears (see p. 51).

2 Place some white wool felt on **1** and jab with the needle.

3 The finished ear will look like this, with a thickness of ¼ in (6 mm).

Continued overleaf ⟶

Instructions

 Place the ears at the attachment position on the head and jab the joins thoroughly.

5 Jab the back of the ears thoroughly too.

6 The finished head will look like this with the ears attached.

 Attach the head to the body

1 Lightly jab some beige wool felt at the position on the body where you are going to attach the head. This will allow you to attach the head without glue.

2 Place the head at the attachment position shown in **1**, and jab thoroughly until it blends into the body.

3 The finished dog will look like this.

For a Miniature Schnauzer

Learn how to create floppy ears, mustaches, and a sitting pose.

→ page 10

Attaching the ears

1 Attach the ears in the same way as for the Welsh corgi (see p. 44).

2 Fold down the ears and jab to attach them to the head.

3 The head will look like this when the ears are attached.

Attaching the mustaches

1 Tear some white wool felt into a thin tuft.

2 Fold the wool felt in two and jab it onto the border formed by the color of the snout.

3 First jab the fold thoroughly.

4 Continue by lightly jabbing the remainder of the mustache to secure it in place.

5 Cut ⅜ in (1.5 cm) from the fold.

6 The finished head will look like this.

Making the sitting pose

1 Use wadding to make the filling for the body (left). Wrap the wadding in gray wool felt, jabbing evenly as you do so (right).

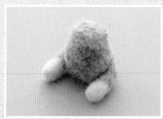

2 Attach the hind legs to the underside of the body.

3 Attach the front legs in a V-shaped formation, with the feet sitting between the hind legs.

4 This is how the finished dog will look with the head and body attached.

For a Toy Poodle

→ page 26

The Toy Poodle is the only dog that uses loop yarn, which gives a fluffy texture like that of curly hair.

1 Use a light brown (or undyed) felting yarn loop.

2 Make the filling for the head with wadding, and then jab the felting yarn loop in a helical pattern.

3 Wrap the entire head evenly and jab.

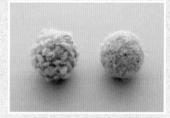

4 The ball on the left has been jabbed across its entire surface. The ball on the right has been jabbed until the loops are obscured.

LET'S GET STARTED!

- →

Making the dogs

🐾 In this section, each of the breeds features an actual-size photograph with details of materials required and assembly instructions.

For more specific, step-by-step guidance on techniques, refer to p. 32 to 46 (where we show you how to make the dogs using the example of the Welsh Corgi).

Use the actual-size photographs to help you work out the sizes.

🐾 The amounts of wool included in the instructions is intended as a guide.

There will be a variance of around $\frac{1}{16}$ oz (2 g) in the amount of wool you use to produce a dog of the same finished size, depending on whether you compact the wool hard or leave it soft and fluffy.

In any case, it makes sense to start with small amounts of wool and gradually add more as you work.

MINIATURE DACHSHUND

→ page 6, 7, and 19

● Materials (red)
Wool felt: Brown (220) x ½ oz (15 g), dark brown (31) x ⅛ oz (5 g)
Wadding: Brown (312) x ½ oz (15 g)
Eyes: Solid (black), ⅛ in (4 mm) x 2
Nose: (Dark brown), ⅜ in (9 mm) x 1
No. 25 embroidery thread: Dark brown, a little

● Materials (black & tan)
Wool felt: Black (9) x ½ oz (15 g), brown (220) x ¼ oz (7 g)
Wadding: Brown (312) x ½ oz (15 g)
Eyes: Flat (light brown), ¼ in (6 mm) x 2
Nose: (Black), ⅜ in (9 mm) x 1
No. 25 embroidery thread: Black, a little

Actual size

Red   **Black & tan**

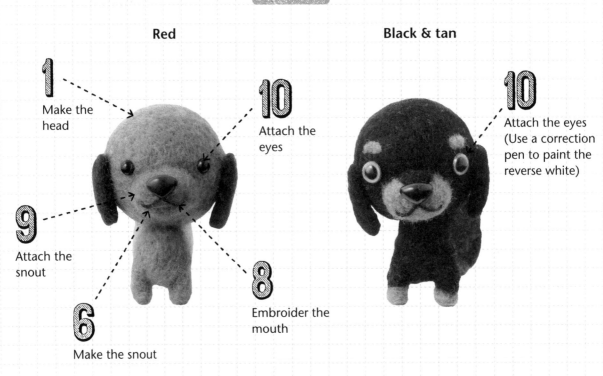

1 Make the head

10 Attach the eyes

9 Attach the snout

6 Make the snout

8 Embroider the mouth

10 Attach the eyes (Use a correction pen to paint the reverse white)

*For detailed instructions, see p. 35 to 46

● Finished size

Head circumf.	$4^{1}/_{8}$ in (10.5 cm)
Body circumf.	2 in (5 cm)
Body length	$1^{3}/_{4}$ in (4.5 cm)

* See the photographs for the lengths of the other sections and where to attach the eyes, nose, and ears.

❀ NOTE

For the black & tan version, add some brown wool felt to the ends of the legs. Add the black patch above the mouth before you attach the nose. For the eyebrows, shape tiny amounts of wool felt and then attach them to the head. Otherwise, follow the instructions for the red version.

Actual-size pattern for the ears

Actual size

Side-on

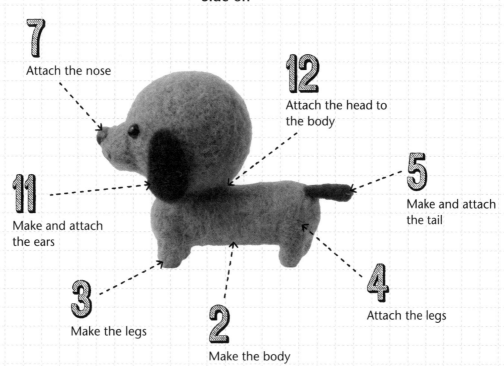

7 Attach the nose

12 Attach the head to the body

11 Make and attach the ears

5 Make and attach the tail

3 Make the legs

2 Make the body

4 Attach the legs

WELSH CORGI

→ page 8, 9, and 19

● **Materials (fawn)**
Wool felt: Beige (803) x ½ oz (15 g), white (1) x ⅛ oz (5 g)
Wadding: Undyed (310) x ½ oz (15 g)
Eyes: Solid (black), ⅛ in (4 mm) x 2
Nose: (Dark brown), ⅜ in (9 mm) x 1
No. 25 embroidery thread: Dark brown, a little

● **Materials (tricolor)**
Wool felt: Black (9) x ½ oz (15 g), beige (803) and white (310) x ⅛ oz (5 g) each
Wadding: Light gray (311) x ½ oz (15 g)
Eyes: Flat (light brown), ¼ in (6 mm) x 2
Nose: (Black), ⅜ in (9 mm) x 1
No. 25 embroidery thread: Black, a little

Actual size

Fawn

Tricolor

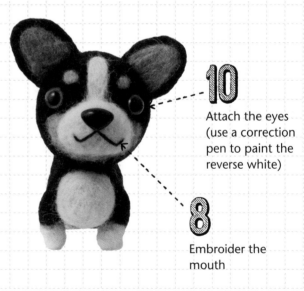

1 Make the head

9 Attach the snout

6 Make the snout

10 Attach the eyes (use a correction pen to paint the reverse white)

8 Embroider the mouth

* For detailed instructions, see p. 35 to 46

● **Finished size**

Head circumf.	4¹/₈ in (10.5 cm)
Body circumf.	2 in (5 cm)
Body length	1³/₄ in (4.5 cm)

* See the photographs for the lengths
of the other sections and where
to attach the eyes, nose, ears, and
eyebrows (on the tricolor version only).

❀ NOTE

For the tricolor version, proceed
in the same way as for the fawn,
except for adding the eyebrows
after you attach the eyes and
adding the marking around the
snout. For the eyebrows, shape
tiny amounts of wool felt and add
them to the head.

Actual-size pattern for the ears

Side-on

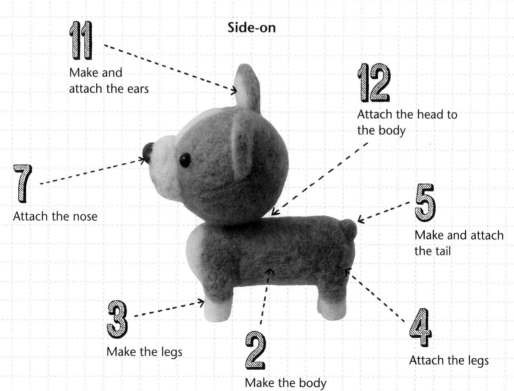

11 Make and attach the ears

12 Attach the head to the body

7 Attach the nose

5 Make and attach the tail

3 Make the legs

4 Attach the legs

2 Make the body

* 1 square = ¼ in (5 mm)   51 ❀

MINIATURE SCHNAUZER

→ page 10, 11, and 18

⬤ **Materials (salt & pepper)**
Wool felt: Mixed gray (805) x ½ oz (15 g), white (1)
x ⅛ oz (5 g)
Wadding: Undyed (310) x ½ oz (15 g)
Eyes: Solid (black), ⅛ in (4 mm) x 2
Nose: (Black), ⅜ in (9 mm) x 1
No. 25 embroidery thread: Black, a little

⬤ **Materials (black & silver)**
Wool felt: Black (9) x ½ oz (15 g), white (1) x ⅛ oz (5 g)
Wadding: Light gray (311) x ½ oz (15 g)
Eyes: Solid (black), ⅛ in (4 mm) x 2
Nose: (Black), ⅜ in (9 mm) x 1
No. 25 embroidery thread: Black, a little

Actual size

Lying down pose

1
Make the head

10
Attach the eyes

11
Make and attach the ears

8
Embroider the mouth

2
Make the body

3
Make the legs

*For detailed instructions, see p. 35 to 46

● Finished size

Head circumf.	4 in (10 cm)
Body circumf.	2³/₈ in (6 cm)
Body length	1³/₄ in (4.5 cm)

* See the photographs for the lengths of the other sections and where to attach the eyes, nose, and ears.

☙ NOTE

Add the gray patch above the mouth before you attach the nose. Add the eyebrows after you attach the eyes. See p. 45 for how to attach the ears and mustaches, and p. 46 for how to create the sitting pose. For a lying down pose, attach the four legs facing forward.

Actual-size pattern for the ears

Actual size

Sitting pose

7 Attach the nose

6 Make the snout

12 Attach the head to the body

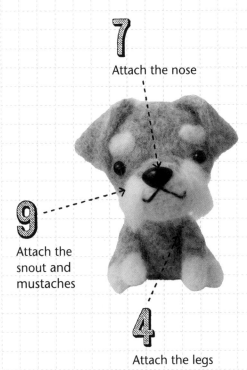

9 Attach the snout and mustaches

4 Attach the legs

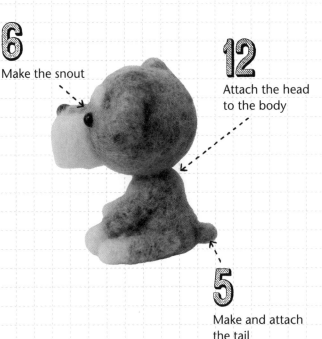

5 Make and attach the tail

PUG

→ page 12, 13, and 18

● **Materials (fawn)**
Wool felt: Ivory (801) x ½ oz (15 g), black (9) x ⅛ oz (5 g)
Wadding: Undyed (310) x ½ oz (15 g)
Eyes: Flat (light brown), ¼ in (6 mm) x 2
Nose: (Black), ⅜ in (9 mm) x 1
No. 25 embroidery thread: Gray, a little

● **Materials (black)**
Wool felt: Black (9) x ¾ oz (20 g)
Wadding: Gray (311) x ½ oz (15 g)
Eyes: Flat (light brown), ¼ in (6 mm) x 2
Nose: (Black), ⅜ in (9 mm) x 1
No. 25 embroidery thread: Gray, a little

Actual size

Fawn/sitting pose

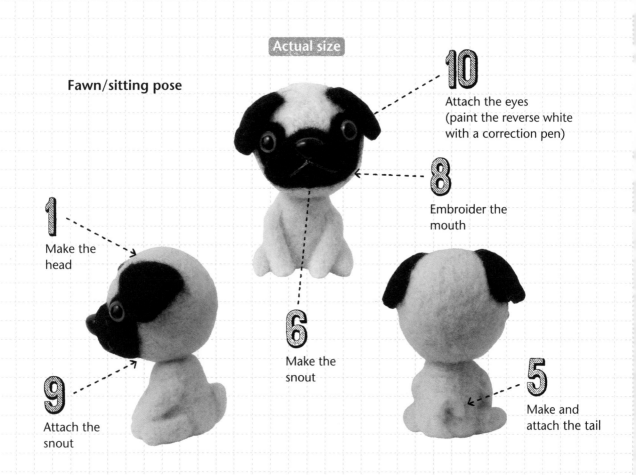

10 Attach the eyes (paint the reverse white with a correction pen)

8 Embroider the mouth

1 Make the head

6 Make the snout

9 Attach the snout

5 Make and attach the tail

*For detailed instructions, see p. 35 to 46

● **Finished size**

Head circumf.   4 1/8 in (10.5 cm)

Body circumf.   2 1/2 in (6.5 cm)

Body length   1 3/4 in (4.5 cm)

* See the photographs for the lengths of the other sections and where to attach the eyes, nose, and ears.

❀ NOTE

See p. 45 for how to attach the ears. For the fawn version, shape and attach a tiny amount of black wool felt to the area around the eyes before you attach the eyes.

Actual-size pattern for the ears

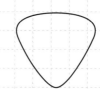

Actual size

Black/standing pose

11
Make and attach the ears

7
Attach the nose

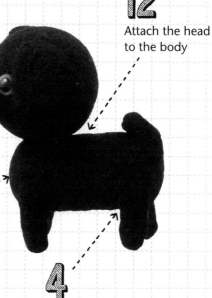

12
Attach the head to the body

3
Make the legs

2
Make the body

4
Attach the legs

* 1 square = 1/4 in (5 mm)   55 ❀

CHIHUAHUA

→ page 14, 15, and 18

● **Materials**
Wool felt: White (1) x ¾ oz (20 g)
Wadding: Undyed (310) x ½ oz (15 g)
Eyes: Solid (black), ¼ in (6 mm) x 2
Nose: (Black), ⅜ in (9 mm) x 1
No. 25 embroidery thread: Black, a little

Actual size

Sitting pose

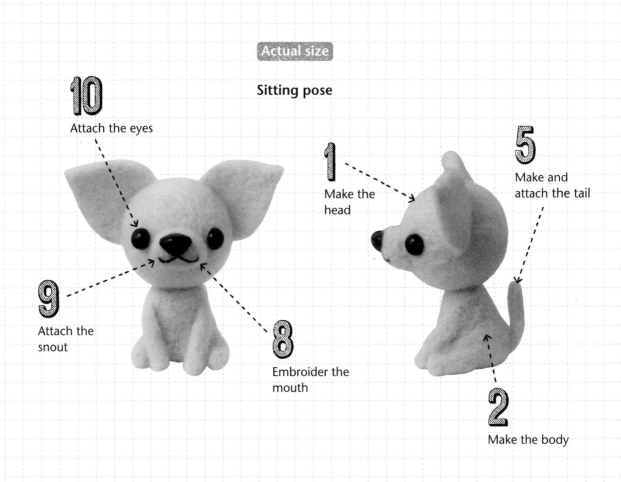

10 Attach the eyes

9 Attach the snout

8 Embroider the mouth

1 Make the head

5 Make and attach the tail

2 Make the body

*For detailed instructions, see p. 35 to 46

● Finished size

Head circumf.   4¹/₈ in (10.5 cm)

Body circumf.   2¹/₂ in (6.5 cm)

Body length   1¹/₈ in (3 cm)

* See the photographs for the lengths of the other sections and where to attach the eyes, nose, and ears.

❀ NOTE

Attach the ears in a curved shape. See p. 46 for how to create a sitting pose. For a lying down pose, attach the four legs facing forward.

Actual-size pattern for the ears

Actual size

Lying down pose

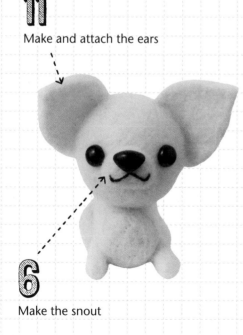

11 Make and attach the ears

6 Make the snout

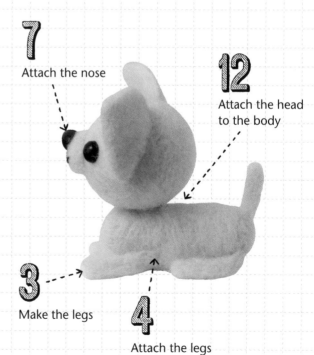

7 Attach the nose

12 Attach the head to the body

3 Make the legs

4 Attach the legs

LABRADOR RETRIEVER

→ page 16, 17, and 19

● **Materials (yellow)**
Wool felt: Cream (42) x ¾ oz (20 g)
Wadding: Undyed (310) x ½ oz (15 g)
Eyes: Solid (black), ⅛ in (4 mm) x 2
Nose: (Black), ⅜ in (9 mm) x 1
No. 25 embroidery thread: Black, a little

● **Materials (black)**
Wool felt: Black (9) x ¾ oz (20 g)
Wadding: Gray (311) x ½ oz (15 g)
Eyes: Flat (light brown), ¼ in (6 mm) x 2
Nose: (Black), ⅜ in (9 mm) x 1
No. 25 embroidery thread: Black, a little

Actual size

Yellow/sitting pose

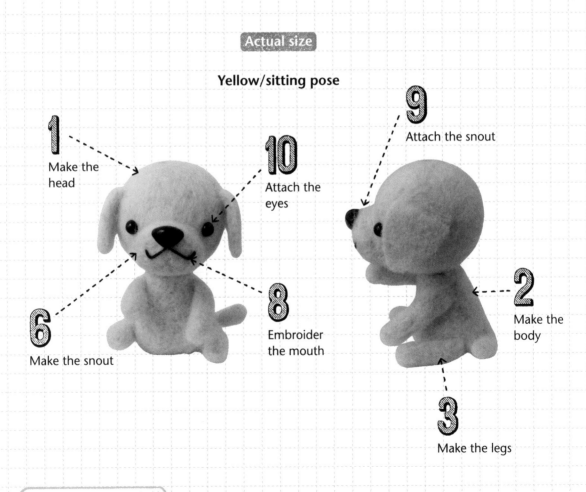

1 Make the head

10 Attach the eyes

9 Attach the snout

6 Make the snout

8 Embroider the mouth

2 Make the body

3 Make the legs

*For detailed instructions, see p. 35 to 46

● **Finished size**

Head circumf. $4^{1}/_{8}$ in (10.5 cm)

Body circumf.(max) $2^{1}/_{2}$ in (6.5 cm)

Body length $1^{3}/_{4}$ in (4.5 cm)

* See the photographs for the lengths
of the other sections and where to
attach the eyes, nose, and ears.

🐾 NOTE

See p. 46 for how to create a
sitting pose. For a beddy-bye pose,
attach the four legs facing forward.

**Actual-size pattern
for the ears**

Actual size

Black/beddy-bye pose

10 Attach the eyes (paint the reverse
white with a correction pen)

11 Make and attach the ears

5 Make and attach
the tail

7 Attach the nose

12 Attach the head to the body

4 Attach the legs

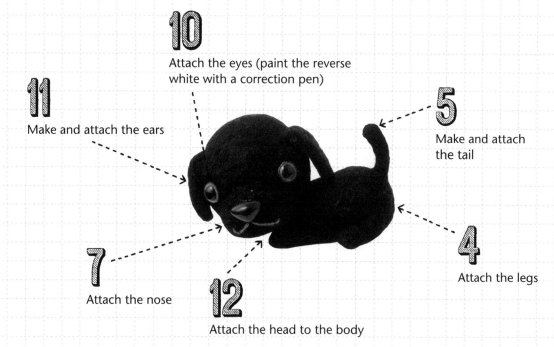

* 1 square = ¼ in (5 mm)

SHIBA

→ page 18, 20, and 21

● **Materials (reddish brown)**
Wool felt: reddish brown (32) x ½ oz (15 g), white (1) x ¼ oz (7 g)
Wadding: Undyed (310) x ½ oz (15 g)
Eyes: Solid (black), ⅛ in (4 mm) x 2
Nose: (Black), ⅜ in (9 mm) x 1
No. 25 embroidery thread: Black, a little

● **Materials (black)**
Wool felt: Black (9) x ½ oz (15 g), white (1) x ⅛ oz (5 g), reddish brown (32) x ⅟₁₆ oz (2 g)
Wadding: Gray (311) x ½ oz (15 g)
Eyes: Flat (light brown), ¼ in (6 mm) x 2
Nose: (Black), ⅜ in (9 mm) x 1

● **Materials (dog bowl)**
Wool felt: Vermilion (16) x ⅛ oz (5 g)

● **Materials (bone)**
Wool felt: White (1) x ⅟₁₆ oz (2 g)

Actual size

Black   Dog bowl

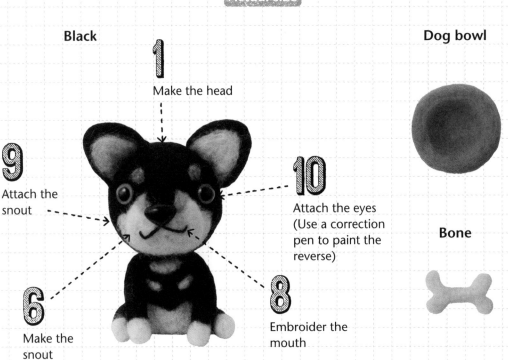

1 Make the head

9 Attach the snout

10 Attach the eyes (Use a correction pen to paint the reverse)

6 Make the snout

8 Embroider the mouth

Bone

*For detailed instructions, see p. 35 to 46

● Finished size

Head circumf.	4 in (10 cm)
Body circumf.	2³/₈ in (6.5 cm)
Body length	1 in (2.5 cm)

* See the photographs for the lengths of the other sections and where to attach the eyes, nose, and ears.

✿ NOTE

Add the differently shaded patch on the snout before you attach the nose. For the reddish brown version, add the white wool felt to the body before you attach the legs and to the eyebrows and underside of the snout after you attach the eyes. For the black version, add the white wool felt to the front part of the body in the form of markings. Add the eyebrows and reddish brown patch above the mouth after you attach the eyes, and then add the white to the underside of the snout. See p. 46 for how to create a sitting pose.

Actual-size pattern for the ears

Actual size

Reddish brown

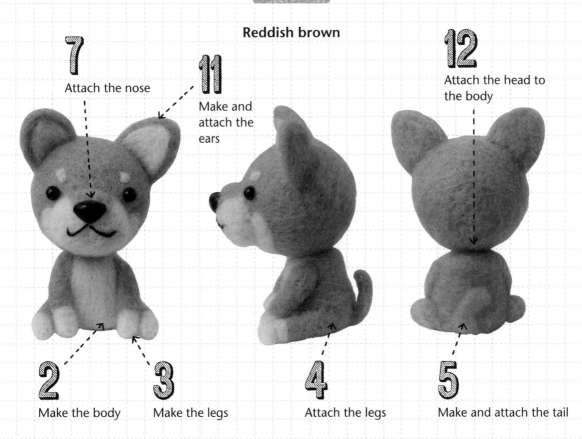

7 Attach the nose

11 Make and attach the ears

12 Attach the head to the body

2 Make the body

3 Make the legs

4 Attach the legs

5 Make and attach the tail

MALTESE

→ page 19, 22, and 23

● **Materials**
Wool felt: White (1) x ¾ oz (20 g)
Wadding: Undyed (310) x ½ oz (15 g)
Eyes: Solid (black), ⅛ in (4 mm) x 2
Nose: (Black), ⅜ in (9 mm) x 1
No. 25 embroidery thread: Black, a little
Decorative ribbon: x 2

Actual size

Sitting pose

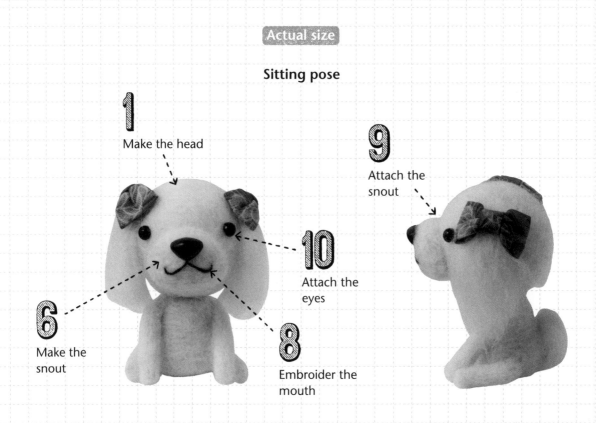

1 Make the head

9 Attach the snout

10 Attach the eyes

6 Make the snout

8 Embroider the mouth

*For detailed instructions, see p. 35 to 46

● Finished size

Head circumf.	$4^1/_8$ in (10.5 cm)
Body circumf.	$2^1/_8$ in (5.5 cm)
Body length	$1^3/_4$ in (4.5 cm)

* See the photographs for the lengths of the other sections and where to attach the eyes, nose, and ears.

❀ NOTE

For how to make and attach the ears, see the instructions on adding mustaches to a Miniature Schnauzer on p. 45. For how to create a sitting pose, see p. 46. For a lying down pose, attach the four legs facing forward. Attach ribbons at the base of the ears.

Actual size

Lying down pose

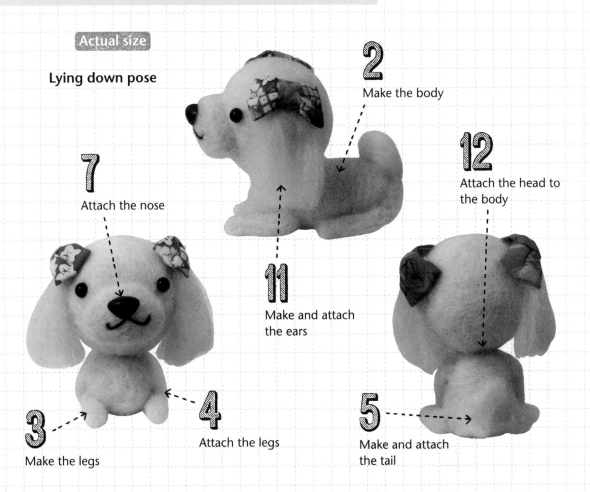

2 Make the body

12 Attach the head to the body

7 Attach the nose

11 Make and attach the ears

3 Make the legs

4 Attach the legs

5 Make and attach the tail

* 1 square = ¼ in (5 mm)   63 ❀

BEAGLE

→ page 18, 24, and 25

● **Materials (adult)**
Wool felt: Brown (220) x ½ oz (13 g), white (1) x ⅛ oz (5 g),
black (9) x ⅛ oz (5 g)
Wadding: Undyed (310) x ½ oz (15 g)
Eyes: Solid (black), ⅛ in (4 mm) x 2
Nose: (Black), ⅜ in (9 mm) x 1
No. 25 embroidery thread: Black, a little

● **Materials (pup)**
Wool felt: Black (9) x ½ oz (12 g), white (1) x ⅛ oz (4 g),
brown (220) x ¹⁄₁₆ oz (3 g)
Wadding: Undyed (310) x ½ oz (13 g)
Eyes: Solid (black), ⅛ in (4 mm) x 2
Nose: (Black), ⅜ in (9 mm) x 1
No. 25 embroidery thread: Black, a little

Actual size

Adult/sitting pose

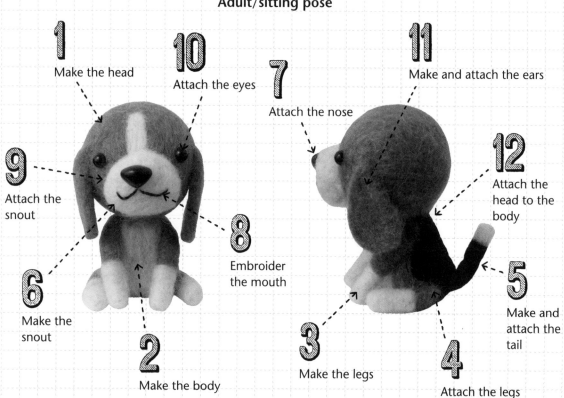

1 Make the head

10 Attach the eyes

7 Attach the nose

11 Make and attach the ears

9 Attach the snout

6 Make the snout

8 Embroider the mouth

2 Make the body

3 Make the legs

4 Attach the legs

5 Make and attach the tail

12 Attach the head to the body

*For detailed instructions, see p. 35 to 46

● Finished size

Head circumf.	$4^1/_8$ in (10.5 cm)
Body circumf.	$2^1/_8$ in (6 cm)
Body length	1 in (2.5 cm)

* Refer to the photographs for size of the pup, the lengths of the other sections on the adult, and where to attach the eyes, nose, and ears.

❀ NOTE

For the sitting pose, add the white wool felt to the front when you make the body. Add the ears pointing down. For the pup, add the stripe to the head, and then the facial markings in brown (with raised circles $1^1/_8$ in [3 cm] in diameter around the eyes only). See p. 46 for how to create a sitting pose. For a lying down pose, attach the four legs facing forward.

Actual-size pattern for the ears

Adult · Pup

Actual size

Pup/sitting pose

Pup/lying down pose

TOY POODLE

→ page 19, 26, and 27

● **Materials (white)**
Felting yarn loop: Undyed (1) x 1 ball
Wadding: Undyed (310) x ½ oz (15 g)
Eyes: Solid (black), ⅛ in (4 mm) x 2
Nose: (Black), ⅜ in (9 mm) x 1
No. 25 embroidery thread: Black, a little

● **Materials (gray)**
Felting yarn loop: Light brown (2) x 1 ball
Wadding: Light gray (311) x ½ oz (15 g)
Eyes: Solid (black), ⅛ in (4 mm) x 2
Nose: (Black), ⅜ in (9 mm) x 1
No. 25 embroidery thread: Black, a little

Actual size

White/lying down pose

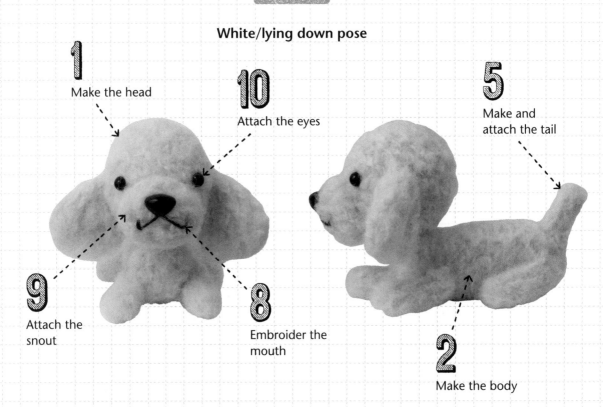

1 Make the head

10 Attach the eyes

5 Make and attach the tail

9 Attach the snout

8 Embroider the mouth

2 Make the body

*For detailed instructions, see p. 35 to 46

● **Finished size**

Head circumf. $4^1/_8$ in (10.5 cm)

Body circumf. $2^1/_8$ in (6 cm)

Body length   2 in (5 cm)

* See the photographs for the lengths of the other sections and where to attach the eyes, nose, and ears.

❀ NOTE

Add felting yarn loop instead of wool felt (see p. 46). See p. 35 to 44 for the other basic techniques.

Actual-size pattern for the ears

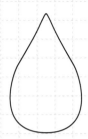

Actual size

Gray/sitting pose

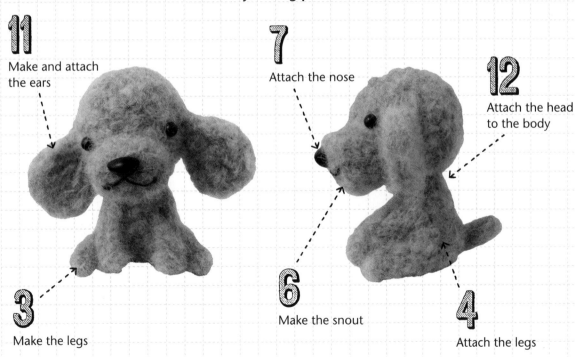

11
Make and attach the ears

7
Attach the nose

12
Attach the head to the body

3
Make the legs

6
Make the snout

4
Attach the legs

BOSTON TERRIER

→ page 18, 28, and 29

● **Materials**

Wool felt: Black (9) x ½ oz (15 g), white (1) x ⅛ oz (5 g), pink (22)
x 1⁄16 in (2 g)
Wadding: Undyed (310) x ½ oz (15 g)
Eyes: Flat (clear), ¼ in (6 mm) x 2
Nose: (Black), ¾ in (9 mm) x 1
No. 25 embroidery thread: Black, a little

Actual size

Sitting pose

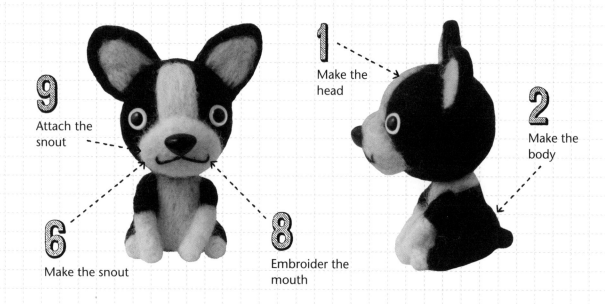

9 Attach the snout

6 Make the snout

8 Embroider the mouth

1 Make the head

2 Make the body

*For detailed instructions, see p. 35 to 46

● **Finished size**

Head circumf. $4^1/8$ in (10.5 cm)

Body circumf. $2^1/8$ in (6 cm)

Body length $1^1/8$ in (3 cm)

* See the photographs for the lengths of the other sections and where to attach the eyes, nose, and ears.

❀ NOTE

Add some white wool felt to the front side and to the back of the neck when you make the body. See p. 46 for how to create a sitting pose. For the beddy-bye pose, attach the head with the face side-on and the four legs facing forward.

Actual-size pattern for the ears

Actual size

Beddy-bye pose

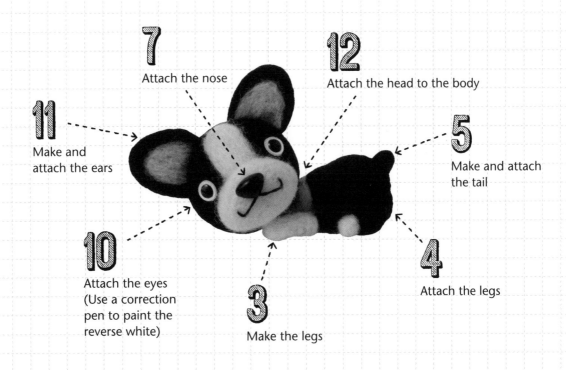

7 Attach the nose

12 Attach the head to the body

11 Make and attach the ears

5 Make and attach the tail

10 Attach the eyes (Use a correction pen to paint the reverse white)

3 Make the legs

4 Attach the legs

* 1 square = $^1/4$ in (5 mm)

MINIATURE PINSCHER

→ page 18, 30, and 31

⬤ **Materials**
Wool felt: Black (9) x ½ oz (15 g), brown (220) x
⅛ oz (5 g)
Wadding: Brown (312) x ½ oz (15 g)
Eyes: Flat (light brown), ¼ in (6 mm) x 2
Nose: (Black), ⅜ in (9 mm) x 1
No. 25 embroidery thread: Black, a little

Lying down pose

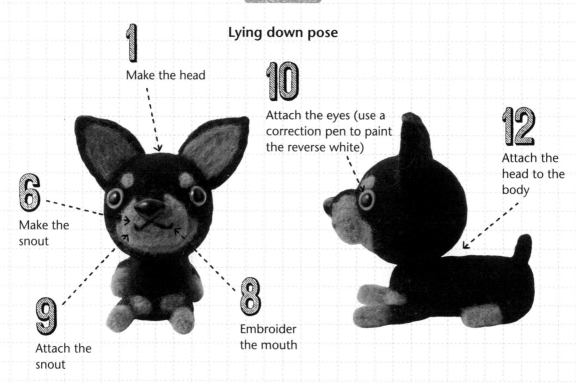

1 Make the head

10 Attach the eyes (use a correction pen to paint the reverse white)

12 Attach the head to the body

6 Make the snout

9 Attach the snout

8 Embroider the mouth

*For detailed instructions, see p. 35 to 46

● Finished size

Head circumf.	4 in (10 cm)
Body circumf.	$2^{1}/_{8}$ in (5.5 cm)
Body length	$1^{3}/_{4}$ in (4.5 cm)

* See the photographs for the lengths of the other sections and where to attach the eyes, nose, and ears.

❀ NOTE

Add some brown wool felt to the chest when you make the body. Add the black patch above the mouth before you attach the nose. After you attach the eyes, add some brown wool felt to the eyebrows and underside of the mouth. One version is in a lying down pose, and another sitting up on its front legs, with the hind legs attached facing forward in both cases.

Actual-size pattern for the ears

Actual size

Sitting pose

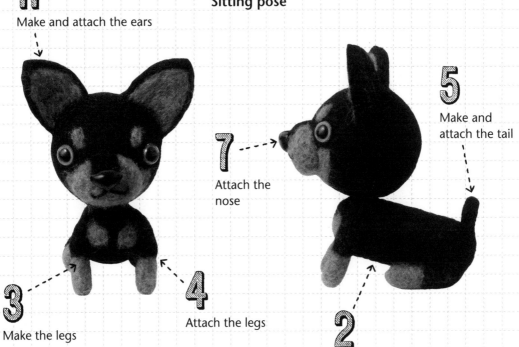

11 Make and attach the ears

7 Attach the nose

5 Make and attach the tail

3 Make the legs

4 Attach the legs

2 Make the body